# Out of the Ice

## How Climate Change Is Revealing the Past

WRITTEN BY Claire Eamer

ILLUSTRATED BY Drew Shannon

KIDS CAN PRESS

For the Yukon ice-patch people, who are so generous with their time and knowledge — C.E.

## Acknowledgments
Thanks to Greg Hare, Don Russell, Kristin Kuzyk, Rae Mombourquette
and Martin Callanan for information and guidance.
Any errors are mine, not theirs.

Text © 2018 Claire Eamer
Illustrations © 2018 Drew Shannon

Kids Can Press gratefully acknowledges the financial support of the Government of Ontario, through the Ontario Media Development Corporation; the Ontario Arts Council; the Canada Council for the Arts; and the Government of Canada, through the CBF, for our publishing activity.

**Photo credits**
Every reasonable effort has been made to trace ownership of and give accurate credit to copyrighted material. Information that would enable the publisher to correct any discrepancies in future editions would be appreciated.

p. 4: Jim Yungel/NASA; p. 7: Yukon Government; p. 9: (left and right) Yukon Government; p. 10: Yukon Government; p. 12: Secrets of the Ice/ Oppland County Council; p. 13: Espen Finstad, secretsoftheice.com; p. 14: (top and bottom) Yukon Government — Ruth Gotthardt; p. 17: Scientific examination of the frozen mummy © South Tyrol Museum of Archaeology/Eurac/Samadelli/Staschitz; p. 19: Jonathan Conville Memorial Trust; p. 20: dpa picture alliance archive/Alamy Stock Photo; p. 23: RGB Ventures/SuperStock/Alamy Stock Photo; p. 25: Vera Salnitskaya/Siberian Times; p. 27: Karen Bear/The Field Museum; p. 28: Shutterstock/Irina Ovchinnikova

Published in Canada and the U.S. by Kids Can Press Ltd.
25 Dockside Drive, Toronto, ON  M5A 0B5

Kids Can Press is a Corus Entertainment Inc. company

www.kidscanpress.com

The artwork in this book was rendered in Graphite, then digitally painted in Adobe Photoshop.
The text is set in Lubalin.

Edited by Stacey Roderick
Designed by Julia Naimska

Printed and bound in Malaysia, in 3/2018 by Tien Wah Press (Pte) Ltd.

CM 18  0 9 8 7 6 5 4 3 2 1

**Library and Archives Canada Cataloguing in Publication**

Eamer, Claire, 1947–, author
    Out of the ice : how climate change is revealing the past / written by Claire Eamer ; illustrated by Drew Shannon.
Includes index.
ISBN 978-1-77138-731-6 (hardcover)

    1. Ice patch archaeology — Juvenile literature.  2. Excavations (Archaeology) — Arctic regions — Juvenile literature.  3. Arctic regions — History — Juvenile literature.  4. Climatic changes — Arctic regions — Juvenile literature.  5. Global warming — Arctic regions — Juvenile literature.  I. Shannon, Drew, 1988–, illustrator II. Title.

CC77.I2E26 2018      j930.1      C2017-907203-X

# Contents

# Frozen in Time

Deep in the massive ice sheet that covers the continent of Antarctica, there is ice that's been around longer than modern humans. Way longer. It froze about 2.7 million years ago, almost a million years before our extinct relatives, a people called *Homo erectus*, were huddling around flickering fires as protection against giant hyenas and enormous, shambling bears. (Our species, *Homo sapiens*, didn't arrive on the scene until a mere 200 000 years ago.)

That's the power of cold. Once water turns to ice, it can stay frozen for a very long time. Anything that's trapped in the ice also stays frozen and preserved — kind of like the veggies in a kitchen freezer.

*The frozen places of the world are melting as Earth's climate changes. And as they melt, the past is revealed.*

And Earth has plenty of frozen water: snow, glaciers, ice patches high in the mountains and the ice that covers lakes and oceans in the world's cold regions. In parts of the world, there's even permanently frozen ground, called *permafrost*, beneath the surface layer of soil. Altogether, those frozen places make up the *cryosphere* (CRY-oh-sfeer), a word derived from the Greek word *kryos*, which means "cold."

Some of the ice lasts for just a season, but some is hundreds or even thousands of years old. And that ice can contain amazing surprises —

tools, weapons, clothing and even the bodies of people who lived long ago. Frozen along with them are bits of the world they lived in, such as plants, animal remains, even layers of dust. These are all clues that can tell us what that world was like.

But now, global climate change is warming Earth's air, ground and water, and some of those frozen clues are melting out of the ice.

The study of this once-frozen material is called *glacial archaeology* (even though it refers to all of the cryosphere, not just glaciers). Archaeologists and other scientists

have been surprised and delighted by these unexpected discoveries even as they scramble to find and preserve the material before it thaws and turns to dust. These relics of the past have stories to tell — stories we're still trying to understand and stories we haven't even imagined.

## Earth as a Greenhouse

When the sun's energy (both heat and light) hits Earth, some is absorbed and some bounces back into space. But Earth's atmosphere contains a few gases, such as carbon dioxide and methane, that stop the energy from escaping. These heat-trapping gases are called *greenhouse gases*, and a lot of them come from human activities, such as farming, industry and the burning of fossil fuels (oil, gas, coal). The more greenhouse gases there are in the atmosphere, the more Earth warms up and the climate changes.

# Mystery on the Mountain

**The place:** Yukon Territory, northwestern Canada
**The date:** August 31, 1997, a sunny day at the end
of an unusually hot summer

Gerry and Kristin Kuzyk were hunting mountain sheep on the bare upper slopes of a mountain called Thandlät. While Gerry peered through his binoculars, searching for a sheep for their winter meat supply, Kristin enjoyed the view. It included an ice patch — a towering mound of snow and ice — almost a kilometer (about half a mile) away. The ice, which had stayed frozen through years of summers, looked dirty. Very dirty. Kristin wondered why, so she and Gerry hiked to the ice patch to take a closer look.

It turned out to be more than dirty. It smelled! Something black and stinky was melting out of the ice.

Up close, the Kuzyks saw that the black guck was actually animal dung, lying on top of the ice, layered through it and oozing out along its downhill edge. It looked — and smelled — as if the animals had been there only days before. As a biologist with the Yukon government, Gerry was pretty sure it was caribou dung. And yet, caribou hadn't been seen on that mountainside in almost 70 years.

*Archaeologists carefully examine an object left behind by melting ice.*

Baffled, Gerry asked one of Canada's top caribou biologists, Don Russell, to visit the ice patch. Don agreed that the black guck was caribou dung. But there was so much of it! Even a large herd would need years to produce so much dung. The stuff had to be older than it looked and smelled. To add to the mystery, Don spotted a stick beside the ice patch, far from where any trees or bushes grew. It had a bit of string wrapped around one end, holding a bedraggled piece of feather.

The biologists packed up the stick and a sample of dung and took them to local archaeologist Greg Hare, hoping that he could help them solve the mystery.

At first, Greg was sure that neither the stick nor the dung was very old, since organic material — stuff that comes from once-living things — rots quickly in Canada's acidic soils. But the string-wrapped stick was especially puzzling. The string was twisted sinew, a kind of tough animal fiber. Greg thought the stick might be part of an arrow dating back as much as a century. To find out, he sent the stick, string and dung to a radiocarbon-dating lab.

*The sinew-wrapped wooden stick found by biologist Don Russell.*

## Radiocarbon Dating

All living things absorb carbon-14 — a special form of the element carbon — from food, water and even the air. Plants and animals stop absorbing carbon-14 when they die, and then the carbon-14 in their remains slowly changes. Carbon-14 is radioactive, which means it has extra electrons that it gets rid of over time. That's why it's often called radiocarbon. By measuring how much of the carbon-14 has shed its extra electrons, scientists can tell how long ago the plant or animal was alive.

# Time Detectives at Work

When the lab results came back, Greg Hare was amazed. The caribou dung was 2400 years old — older than the Roman Empire! And the stick was even older. At 4300 years old, it had been around at the time ancient Britons were building their giant monument, Stonehenge. In fact, when it was discovered, it was one of the oldest organic artifacts (human-made objects) ever to be found in Canada.

Archaeologists love organic artifacts. That's partly because radiocarbon dating can pinpoint the age of organic material to within a few decades. Determining the age of stone or metal artifacts is much harder because the material doesn't change over time.

*An archaeologist uses a chain saw to slice out a section of compressed ice. Each layer is a step back in time.*

But organic material contains other information, too. A stick can tell you what sort of tree once grew nearby. Dung can tell you what long-dead animals ate. A feather tied to a wooden shaft can tell you when a hunter lived and how he made his weapons.

Frozen organic material can survive almost unchanged for thousands of years. But once it thaws, it doesn't last long. Animal poop crumbles to dust in weeks or months, and a stick might last a few years at most before it decomposes. The Yukon ice patch was a kind of time capsule, but it was in danger: global climate change was making Yukon summers warmer and shrinking the ice patches. Anything melting out of them might disintegrate before it could be discovered and studied.

By the time the radiocarbon lab results for the dung and the stick had come back, it was already winter. That meant the Yukon researchers had to wait until the following summer to begin scouring the mountains for more ice patches with caribou dung. Since then, they've found another 42 ice patches that contain animal remains and artifacts — everything from dung and feathers to broken sticks, beautifully carved bone and antler spear points, and the oldest moccasin found in Canada, which was worn and lost 1300 years ago.

Before the Yukon discoveries, no one suspected that ice patches might hold ancient relics. Now, people are searching ice patches elsewhere and finding more evidence of the past — in neighboring Alaska and the Northwest Territories, and farther south, in British Columbia, Colorado and Wyoming.

*The oldest moccasin found in Canada looked like a lump of old leather when discovered.*

## The Signature of a Long-Ago Artist

**Once upon a time in the Yukon, someone — probably a man, since hunting and making weapons were usually men's work — spent days turning a caribou antler into a deadly dart point. He whittled it flat and pointed at one end. On each side of the point, he glued thin, sharp wafers of stone into narrow grooves to make cutting edges. Finally, on the side of the point, he carved an elegant spiral twisting around a straight line, perhaps as his personal mark or signature. Eventually, he lost the dart point on an ice patch, where it was found 8000 years later, still beautiful and deadly.**

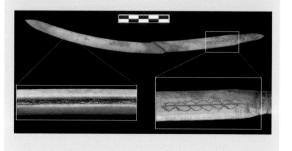

# Hunters, Arrows and Atlatls

The artifacts from the North American ice patches show that people had hunted there for thousands of years. And it makes sense. The hunters were following caribou that retreated to patches of ice and snow during the summer to escape the swarms of mosquitoes and biting flies. The cold air kept the bugs away while the caribou ate, rested and, of course, pooped. And since hunting is hard work, the hunters didn't waste much energy searching for lost or broken gear. Today, that long-frozen gear is telling us their stories.

The oldest story comes from the Yukon, where some of the artifacts were lost in the ice more

than 9000 years ago. Most of the oldest finds are broken bits of stick. But they aren't arrows, as Greg Hare first thought. They're darts, or lightweight spears that were launched from a throwing stick, which is often called an *atlatl* (at-LA-tul). The atlatl itself is a stick or narrow board with a small hook near one end. The hook fits into a dimple carved into the base of the dart. A dart can go much farther and faster thrown from an atlatl than thrown by hand.

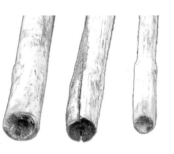

*The dimples (or indentations) in the bottoms of these shafts identify them as atlatl darts, not arrows.*

*A hunter using an atlatl can accurately throw a dart a great distance at his prey.*

Don Russell's 4300-year-old broken stick — with its telltale dimple in one end — was the first organic evidence of atlatl use found in the Yukon. Because of it and other artifacts found in the ice patches, we know that Yukon hunters used atlatls and darts for thousands of years.

We also know all this changed about 1200 years ago, around the time a huge volcano erupted, spreading a thick blanket of ash over the southern Yukon. The ash buried plants, killed or drove animals away and probably forced people to leave the region to find food. The ice-patch layers from the following years are virtually empty of animal remains and artifacts.

Eventually, people returned, bringing a new technology with them. After the volcanic eruption, the sticks left behind in the ice were arrows, with notches for bowstrings instead of dimples for atlatl hooks. These people were bow hunters. Maybe the atlatl hunters had met some bow hunters and learned a new way of doing things. Or maybe an entirely new group of people had moved to the Yukon. We'll never know for sure, but we do know when the technology changed, thanks to the melting ice patches.

## Calling in the Experts

**Understanding the artifacts in the ice patches takes more than science. It also takes the traditional knowledge of local Indigenous elders. Even if they personally have never hunted on the ice patches, elders recognize traditional tools used for processing meat and hides. Some even played with homemade bows and throwing sticks as children and can show the scientists exactly how to make and use them.**

# Vikings on the Mountains

Hikers have been finding hunting artifacts in the Norwegian mountains since 1914 — arrowheads, broken shafts, fragments of bows and even early guns and bullets. A few artifacts were radiocarbon dated, and the oldest came from about 1700 years ago. Most archaeologists assumed that these objects had been dropped by long-ago travelers.

But global warming has been melting Norwegian ice patches, too. Over a series of warm summers, starting in 2001, more artifacts began to appear, and they were older. A slate arrowhead, found in 2006 and dated by analyzing the organic glue that held it to its shaft, was 4300 years old. That's the same age as the atlatl dart Don Russell found in the Yukon.

By the time older artifacts began appearing, Norwegian researchers had heard about the ice-patch hunters of the Yukon. They started looking at their own melting patches with fresh eyes. The evidence of ancient hunting was there.

In fact, in at least one place, ice-patch hunting had been big business. Evidence showed that large groups of people had hunted entire herds of reindeer. They set up rows of sewels, or scaring sticks, made from thin poles, with wood or leather attachments that flopped about in the breeze. Then some of the hunters hid behind low stone walls called hunting blinds, which can still be seen in some ice patches. The rows of sewels acted as a funnel leading toward the blinds. (In a few places, archaeologists have found lines of sewels still jammed into the ice and rock.) A few hunters chased the reindeer into the funnel, where the flapping of the sewels frightened the animals enough to stop them from escaping. Once the reindeer were close to the blinds, the waiting hunters started shooting.

The days when whole villages turned out to hunt reindeer on Norwegian ice patches are long gone, lost to memory. But today, the melting ice is revealing to modern Norwegians the forgotten cleverness and skill of their ancestors.

*Ancient scaring sticks found in Norway.*

## The Mysterious Behavior of Ice Patches

**Scientists are beginning to suspect that mountain ice patches are more complicated than they first thought. In Norway, the ice patches are melting layer by layer, revealing older and older material with each layer. The Yukon ice patches, on the other hand, are melting around the edges so that the exposed ice from all time periods melts at once.**

# Lost on the Glacier

Mountain ice patches aren't the only kind of ice that's revealing important archaeological finds. In the hot summer of 1999, three hunters walking beside the edge of a melting glacier in northwestern Canada discovered evidence of a long-forgotten tragedy: a young man, long dead, his body just beginning to emerge from the ice.

Judging by the possessions scattered nearby, he had probably lived before Europeans had reached that part of North America. Since he was Indigenous, the Champagne and Aishihik First Nations — whose territory he was found in — took responsibility for the body. They called him Kwädąy Dän Ts'ìnchį, meaning "long-ago person found."

Glaciers move and flow with such power that anything trapped in them can be crushed or broken. In Kwädąy Dän Ts'ìnchį's case, his body had been torn in half and his head was missing. Nevertheless, researchers managed to piece together his story.

*The tight weave of Kwädąy Dän Ts'ìnchį's spruce-root hat would have been good protection from both sun and rain.*

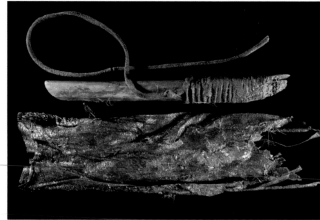

*This knife and ground-squirrel sheath were found with Kwädąy Dän Ts'ìnchį's remains.*

knife, a walking stick and a beaver-skin pouch.

A couple of days into the journey, something had gone terribly wrong — maybe he fell, slipped into a crevice in the ice or was caught in a blizzard — and he died. The snow that covered him turned to ice, preserving his body, his possessions and his story.

Scientists were able to analyze the DNA (genetic material specific to each person) from Kwädąy Dän Ts'ìnchi̠'s frozen and well-preserved bones and internal organs. They compared it to DNA from people in the region and found 17 living relatives of the young man, including members of the Champagne and Aishihik First Nations. Today, Kwädąy Dän Ts'ìnchi̠ is back on the glacier, having been cremated and buried in a traditional ceremony.

His bone development told them he was about 18 years old at the time of his death, and radiocarbon dating showed he had lived between 1720 and about 1850. His bones also told them he had grown up near the ocean. The food you eat leaves traces in your bones, and Kwädąy Dän Ts'ìnchi̠'s bones showed he had eaten seafood for most of his life. They also showed that during his last year, he had eaten land-based food such as caribou, moose and sheep, so he had probably spent much of that year inland.

In his stomach, scientists found the remains of foods from the sea and seashore, as well as fruit that ripens in late summer. They deduced that the young man's last journey had probably begun in August near the ocean in what is now Alaska. Judging from where he was found, he had been walking inland into the mountains. He had a woven spruce-root hat to keep off the rain, wore a robe made from 95 ground-squirrel pelts, and carried a

## Ice Patch or Glacier — What's the Difference?

**The main difference between an ice patch and a glacier is size. Ice patches can be as big as several football fields, but glaciers are huge. For example, the Hubbard Glacier in Alaska covers an area larger than the state of Rhode Island. Ice patches melt and grow as the seasons change, but they always stay in the same place. Glaciers are so big and heavy that they actually flow downhill like giant, slow-moving rivers.**

# Traveler from the Past

The most famous glacier discovery to date was made in the mountains between Italy and Austria in 1991, a few years before the Yukon's melting ice patches revealed how much history is preserved in Earth's cryosphere. Two Germans on a late summer hike cut through a gully wet with glacial meltwater and spotted something half encased in ice — a corpse. The man had clearly been dead for some time. His body was shriveled and leathery. Maybe he had been the victim of a climbing accident, they thought. The hikers reported the find to authorities, launching a scientific detective story.

The dead man was not, as it turned out, a recent accident victim. According to radiocarbon dating, he had lived well over 5000 years ago (between 3350 and 3100 BCE). The body was complete, mummified by the dry cold of the high mountains. And it was surrounded by clothing and gear.

Today, the man is known as the Iceman or Ötzi (named for the Ötztal Alps, where he died). His body and possessions were so well preserved by the ice that scientists are still discovering new information from them.

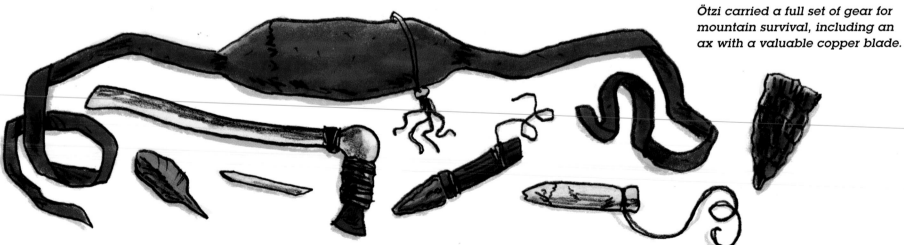

*Ötzi carried a full set of gear for mountain survival, including an ax with a valuable copper blade.*

Ötzi's bones told them that he was about 45 years old and 1.6 m (5 ft. 3 in.) tall, roughly average for his time. His health had not been great — he had tooth decay, worn joints and worms. His last meal included meat, vegetables and either porridge or bread (scientists are still working on that one).

Ötzi wore a bearskin hat, a coat made of goat and sheep skins, goatskin leggings and leather shoes stuffed with grass for warmth. He carried a backpack, a copper-bladed ax, a dagger, tools for fixing his gear, a fire-lighting kit and a couple of birchbark containers. Inside one container were leaves and traces of charcoal, so it had probably held hot embers for starting a fire quickly. He also had a bow and a deerskin quiver of arrows, most of which were broken or unfinished. He might have been making or repairing arrows when he died.

Plant pollen found on his body tells us it was late spring or early summer when Ötzi's journey ended. A deep wound in his hand shows he had been in a fight. He had an arrow in his shoulder and a fractured skull from a blow or fall. Ötzi's last moments were probably full of pain and fear as he fled an enemy we'll never identify.

Hiding in a gully, he leaned his bow against a rock and placed his quiver on a stone slab. Then he lay down or collapsed and died. Soon he was buried in snow, and then ice. For more than 5000 years, Ötzi's body and gear lay in a deep, quiet pool of ice, sheltered by the rock walls of the gully while the glacier grew and flowed above him.

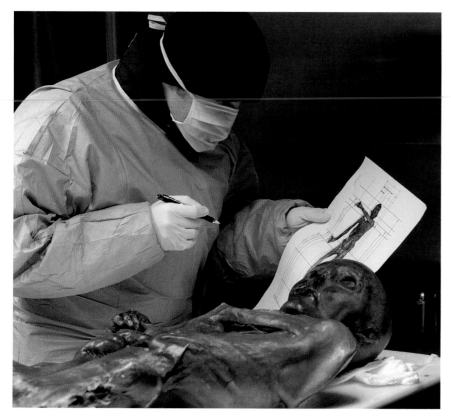

*Ötzi's body is kept frozen to preserve it, so scientists have to bundle up when they study him.*

## What's a Mummy?

**A mummy is the body of a person or animal that has been preserved by drying. Mummification can take place naturally in extremely cold or dry conditions where the bugs and microbes that cause decomposition can't do their work. When that happens, all kinds of information can be preserved in teeth, bones, flesh, internal organs and even stomach contents.**

# Glacial Changes

As the world warms, the extra-hot summers that melted Yukon and Norwegian ice patches and left Ötzi lying in a pool of glacial meltwater are becoming more common. In many parts of the world, melting glaciers are revealing evidence of fairly modern history, as well as the ancient past.

The Matterhorn is a mountain that sticks up like a huge pointed tooth on the border between Italy and Switzerland. Since it was first climbed in 1865, more than 500 people have died on it. Some of the bodies are still there, locked in the mountain's now-shrinking glaciers. In 2013, one of those lost climbers was finally found.

That fall, a helicopter pilot delivering a load of concrete to a mountain hut spotted clothes and climbing gear at the foot of a glacier. Inside the clothing was a body, mostly bones. A name tag on the clothing read "Conville." Bettina Schrag, the scientist examining the remains, searched for the name on the internet and found that a British man named Jonathan Conville had gone missing on the Matterhorn in early 1979. He was 27 years old at the time, an ex-paratrooper and a passionate climber. Caught in bad weather, he fell to his death near the top of the mountain. His body must have been trapped in the glacier, and for 34 years the ice carried him slowly down the mountainside.

To confirm his identity, scientists compared DNA from the remains with samples from Jonathan's two younger sisters, Melissa and Katrina. By the time his body was found, his grieving parents had died, but his sisters were finally able to say a proper farewell to their brother.

Similar stories are becoming increasingly common as the world's melting glaciers give up their dead. Bodies of climbers, hikers, soldiers and tourists who died just decades ago have emerged from glaciers in Europe, Asia, New Zealand and the Americas. And the science that told us so much about Kwädąy Dän Ts'ìnchį and Ötzi is also helping identify the more recent dead and return them to their families.

*Jonathan Conville successfully made many difficult climbs before the one that killed him.*

## The Lost Plane

**In Alaska, an entire airplane — with its passengers — is slowly melting out of a glacier. The plane crashed on Colony Glacier in November 1952, with 52 American Armed Forces members aboard. By the time rescuers reached the wreckage, it had been covered by ice and snow and buried in the glacier. Now, Colony Glacier is melting, retreating up to 300 meters (985 feet) a year. In 2012, bits of wreckage appeared at its edge, with more appearing each year since. All that scientists need to identify the victims is a bit of organic material roughly the weight of three paperclips, and so by the spring of 2016, 32 of the dead have been identified.**

# Lords and Ladies in the Ice

On the high, cold plateaus of the Altai Mountains of central Asia, it's not glaciers or ice patches that preserve the past. It's permafrost.

About 2500 years ago, the Altai Mountains were the territory of the Scythians, a wealthy nomadic people who traveled back and forth across Asia, trading with powerful nations, such as China, India and Persia. Until fairly recently, however, we knew very little about them. They left no written records, and they didn't build cities or fortresses. But they did build tombs.

The Scythian tombs, called kurgans, don't look like much from the outside — just round, shallow holes in the earth, roofed with wood or stone and then covered with piles of rocks. They were dug in the ground where permafrost is close to the surface. Rain and melted snow seeped through the stones and froze, enclosing the kurgans' contents in ice and preserving material that would otherwise have rotted away. The result is a frozen time capsule of a whole way of life.

The people buried in the kurgans were the rich and powerful. These lords and, sometimes, ladies of the Scythian world were entombed with symbols of their wealth and status, such as horses that were killed at the site and buried with their saddles, harnesses and golden headdresses. One kurgan — probably the grave of an especially important leader — held the remains of 16 horses. The dead were left dressed in fine clothing of wool and silk and surrounded by armor, weapons, jewelry, beautifully crafted dishes and decorations made of wood, bone or precious metals. One tomb contained more than 5600 objects made from gold.

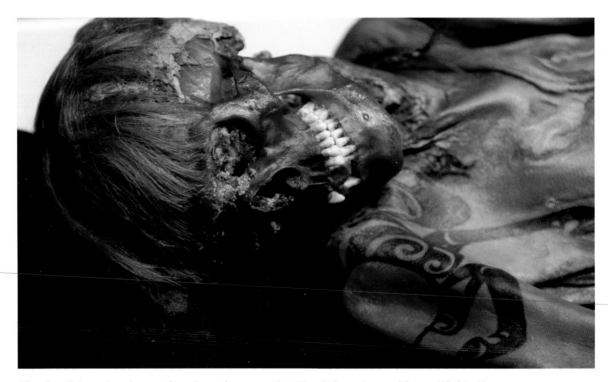

*The Scythian dead are often found covered with elaborate and beautiful tattoos.*

For an archaeologist, these grave goods are loaded with information. For example, wood can be dated — sometimes to a particular year — by analyzing the tree's growth rings. Silk clothing means there was trade with China, the source of silk cloth at that time. The artwork shows influences from India, Persia and even Greece. The weapons and horse gear tell us what technologies the Scythians used.

Up to six human bodies have been found buried together in large kurgans. DNA links them to people living in modern-day Siberia, Kazakhstan and far-western China. A study of hair samples revealed that the Scythians ate a lot of fish. It also showed that they worked with copper: some of the dead had inhaled poisonous copper vapor that left traces in their hair.

There's still more to learn — if the kurgans survive. Global warming threatens to thaw the permafrost in parts of the Altai Mountains, and once thawed, the ancient bodies and organic artifacts will rot away.

## What Is Permafrost?

**High in the mountains or near the North and South Poles, the ground is so cold that any moisture in it freezes and stays frozen year-round. The top layer might thaw in summer, but not far below is the permafrost — ground that never thaws. Or it didn't use to. Now climate change is making it much less permanent than we once thought.**

# Children of the Gods

On the highest peaks of the Andes Mountains, the air is dry, thin and always cold. That's where a special group of frozen bodies has been found — children left as offerings to the gods of the Incas, whose empire covered most of western South America until Spanish invaders arrived in 1532.

According to accounts written after the Spanish invasion, children chosen for their beauty and purity were sacrificed in a ceremony called *capacocha*. Usually, there would be a girl on the brink of becoming a woman, as well as a younger boy and girl, possibly meant as her

servants or companions. The Incas believed that after death, the children would become messengers to the gods and bring the empire good fortune.

The first group of sacrificed children was found in Peru in 1995, but the best-preserved group of bodies was discovered in 1999 in Argentina, on an extinct volcano called Mount Llullaillaco. There, about 6.7 km (4 mi.) above sea level, archaeologists found the frozen bodies of a girl about 13 years old and a younger girl and boy, both between 4 and 5.

*Ceremonial containers and a child's sandals were among the objects found with the Inca children.*

The children had been buried in small pits in the rock. Volcanic ash was packed around and over them, and a stone platform had been built above their graves. The body of the younger girl had been damaged by lightning — always a danger in the high mountains. But the other children were so well preserved that the older girl looked as if she had just fallen asleep. The boy's body had been wrapped and tied in a bundle after he was dead, but the girls were left sitting in their tombs, wrapped in wool shawls.

Scientists have been studying the bodies and the artifacts left with them, reconstructing a picture of the children's lives and their world. When they died, all three had been well fed and generally healthy, although the older girl had a sinus infection and a runny nose. They were dressed in fine clothing and surrounded by possessions and offerings: woven sandals, pottery and small statues dressed in Incan clothing.

Analysis of the children's hair showed that they had all been given alcohol and drugs over the months before they died. None showed obvious signs of injury. Perhaps — cold, tired and woozy from drugs and the thin mountain air — they simply fell asleep and died without waking.

## Voices from the Past

**New ways of analyzing fragile ancient DNA reveal information about the people of the Incan empire and their links to modern people. Powerful new scanners have allowed scientists to see inside the bodies without destroying them. And analysis of the children's gut microbes is telling us about disease, immunity, diet and how we humans have changed — or not changed — over the centuries.**

# A Frozen Zoo

Archaeology isn't just about people. It's also about the world they lived in. And in a few places, that world has been preserved in spectacular detail. One of those places is an area called Beringia, which stretches from northwestern Canada across Alaska and Siberia.

Twenty-five thousand years ago, when huge glaciers covered most of North America and much of Europe and Asia, Beringia was a very special place. Back then, the Bering Strait, which now separates Alaska and Siberia, was a land bridge linking grass-covered plains that were home to a whole menagerie of strange animals: woolly mammoths, huge steppe bison, woolly rhinos, giant short-faced bears and long-toothed scimitar cats. Permafrost lay not far below the surface, and when animals died, their bodies sometimes froze before they could rot away.

The permafrost is still there, but when it's disturbed, it starts to thaw and exposes those ancient bodies. At least 16 species of ice-age mammals — from ground squirrels to woolly mammoths — have been found frozen and mummified in Beringian permafrost.

Some were just babies, such as Uyan and Dina, named after Siberia's Uyandina River, which flooded in the summer of 2015 and washed away part of its bank, exposing a patch of ice. Frozen in the ice were two small, furry bodies about the size of hefty house cats — twin cave-lion cubs, members of a species that became extinct about 10 000 years ago.

*This cave-lion cub lived only weeks before it was covered in mud and frozen thousands of years ago.*

The cubs were only a couple of weeks old when they died, so young that their baby teeth hadn't grown in yet. Their bodies were dried and caked with dirt, but still covered with soft, yellow-brown baby fur. Even their eyes and whiskers survived. Scientists think a landslide covered their den at least 12 000 years ago. The water

and dirt around them froze and stayed frozen, preserving the bodies.

Until Uyan and Dina were discovered, everything we knew about cave lions came from a few bones and from drawings people left on cave walls. Now an international team of experts is studying one of the cubs. The other will be kept frozen and untouched so that future scientists can study it when new scientific tools are developed.

The researchers want to know how long ago the cubs lived and how cave lions are related to other hunting cats. They think the cubs' stomachs might still contain some of their mother's milk. If so, it will reveal a lot about the adult cave lion as well as the babies. It might even help us understand why cave lions became extinct.

## When Did Dogs Become Dogs?

**In 2016, scientists conducted an autopsy on the body of a three-month-old puppy that had died 12 460 years ago. A year earlier, hunters looking for mammoth bones had spotted its nose sticking out of a frozen riverbank in northern Russia. Scientists plan to compare the puppy's DNA to that of modern dogs and wolves to figure out where it fits in the line of dog evolution. We know that dogs evolved from wolves, but we don't know when and where that happened. The ancient puppy from the permafrost might hold an important clue.**

# Mammoths and People

Woolly mammoths are the most famous ice-age animals, and not just because they're often seen in cartoons and on toy shelves. We know a lot about them because of melting permafrost. Mammoth tusks, teeth and bones have been found in northern Russia and northwestern North America for centuries, but

recently, several extremely well-preserved mammoth bodies have melted out of the Russian permafrost.

One was Yuka, a female who died 39 000 years ago when she was no more than nine years old. Her frozen body was found in 2010 near the north coast of Siberia. Unhealed scratches on her hide and

bite marks on her tail suggest that she might have been chased by cave lions. The permafrost had even preserved Yuka's brain. Scientists say its structure is very similar to that of a modern elephant, even though mammoths and elephants became separate species about seven million years ago.

*Baby Lyuba, safely behind glass, now travels the world and introduces people to her species, the woolly mammoth.*

Cave lions didn't kill baby Lyuba. The little mammoth stumbled into a mud hole in northern Siberia about 42 000 years ago and was smothered, her small trunk blocked by sediment. She was barely a month old and the size of a large dog. Mud and water protected the body from organisms that cause decay, and the permafrost kept her frozen — until the young sons of a reindeer herder found her body in the spring of 2007.

Since then, scientists have been studying Lyuba. They've analyzed her DNA and examined her internal organs. Her teeth told them her age and that she had been born in late spring. Her stomach still held traces of her mother's milk, as well as dung from adult mammoths. Why was she eating dung? Elephant mothers today feed bits of dung to their infants to pass on the bacteria they need to digest food, and it appears mammoth mothers did the same thing.

We might learn as much about humans as about mammoths from a third discovery: a male woolly mammoth found in northwestern Russia in 2012 and nicknamed Zhenya after the 11-year-old boy who discovered him. Mammoth Zhenya died 45 000 years ago when he was 15 years old, and Russian scientists think he was killed by human hunters. His bones have marks on them that look like cuts from sharp spear points, and his body bears puncture-like wounds that could have been made by heavy spears after Zhenya had collapsed to the ground.

We already knew that humans hunted mammoths. Ancient artists drew pictures of mammoth hunts on the walls of caves, and we've even found a few sites where the killing took place. But Zhenya tells us something new. If he fell prey to human hunters (and not everyone agrees that he did), then people were living and hunting in Arctic Asia 15 000 years earlier than we thought. In other words, a Russian boy's discovery of a long-dead mammoth could actually rewrite part of human history.

## DNA Prospectors

**Mammoths left their DNA on the landscape in the form of dung, urine, hair and even shed skin cells. In Alaska and the Yukon, researchers are drilling samples of permafrost and analyzing them for woolly mammoth DNA. And they're striking DNA gold. The results show that woolly mammoths survived in Alaska until at least 10 500 years ago, well after they disappeared elsewhere in North America.**

# Slip-Sliding Away

**A**mazingly, there's even more information locked in Earth's cryosphere than can be found in frozen mummies, ancient artifacts and extinct animals. The ice and permafrost hold other evidence of long-lost worlds. Of course, most of it isn't as easy to spot as a woolly mammoth or a delicately carved spear point. In fact, most of it isn't even visible to the naked eye. But it's important just the same.

Every layer of snow that turns into ice and every layer of mud that freezes into permafrost carries bits of the world that formed it — ash from a volcanic eruption, soot from a long-forgotten forest fire, or plant seeds and pollen blown on the wind. DNA has even been found from creatures, besides woolly mammoths, that roamed that bit of the world 1000, 10 000 or 100 000 years ago.

The ice patches, glaciers and permafrost of the cryosphere have recorded a huge chunk of our planet's history, up to 2.7 million years of it in the ice sheets of Antarctica alone. And we are just beginning to learn how to read that record.

But the cryosphere is melting and shrinking, and the frozen record is slip-sliding away with the meltwater. It's not happening all at once. In years when the summers are cool, the ice patches even grow a bit, the glaciers don't melt as quickly and the permafrost stays hard and frozen. But there are fewer cool summers than there used to be and more summers of record-breaking heat. Some small ice patches have disappeared completely in the last couple of decades. Glaciers have shrunk by many kilometers (or miles) or broken off in huge chunks to float away on the ocean as icebergs. Permafrost-rich soil is turning to mud and slumping into rivers and the sea.

Every year, glacial archaeologists and others studying the cryosphere watch the ice patches, glaciers and permafrost closely to see what might be given up. And they scramble to find and preserve those discoveries before both the ice and the knowledge it contains disappear forever.

## The Past Is Us

It may feel as if Kwädąy Dän Ts'ìnchį, Ötzi, the Incan children, the Scythian lords and the hunters on the ice patch belong to a far different time. And they did. But they are also part of what made our world, and so are part of the present, too. Kwädąy Dän Ts'ìnchį's living relatives helped give him, finally, a proper burial. Some of the researchers studying the Incan children are themselves descendants of the Incas. Norwegian archaeologists are just beginning to realize what clever hunters their ancestors were. And the young Indigenous research assistants who help patrol the Yukon ice patches may well be the many-times-great grandchildren of the people who left exquisite weapons behind. Glacial archaeology is allowing us to know those people of the past — of our own past.

# Glossary

**artifact:** an object made by humans

**carbon:** a chemical element that exists in all living things on Earth

**cryosphere:** the places on Earth where water is frozen, either as ice or snow

**First Nations:** Canadian term for the descendants of the original inhabitants of much of what is now Canada. In the United States, the equivalent terms are *Native Americans* or *American Indians.*

**glacier:** a slow-moving mass of ice that is formed by many years of snowfall turned to ice by time and pressure

**ice patch:** a patch of ice and snow that doesn't entirely melt in summer and doesn't flow like a glacier. Found on high mountains in some parts of the world, it is sometimes also called a snow patch.

**ice sheet:** a huge glacier or combinations of glaciers that cover very large areas, such as Antarctica or Greenland

**indigenous:** originating in a place. It often refers to groups of people, as in "The Incas are indigenous people of the Andes."

**organic:** something that is or was alive. The opposite is *inorganic.*

**permafrost:** permanently frozen ground beneath a top layer of dirt. Permafrost is sometimes hundreds of meters (or yards) deep.

**pollen:** powdery material produced by plants and released to drift in the air or cling to passing animals. It contains the plants' male reproductive cells.

**radiocarbon dating:** a method of determining the age of organic material by measuring changes to the carbon-14 in the material

---

# Further Information

**The Frozen Past: The Yukon Ice Patches**, by the Government of Yukon. A well-illustrated online book about discoveries on the Yukon ice patches and what they mean to archaeology and to Yukon people. You can find it at www.tc.gov.yk.ca/publications/The_Frozen_Past_the_Yukon_Ice_Patches_2011.pdf.

**The South Tyrol Museum of Archaeology**: This museum in Italy is the last resting place of Ötzi, the Iceman. Its website is full of information about the discovery and the research, along with plenty of photos and drawings. Find it at www.iceman.it.

**Teachings from Long Ago Person Found: Highlights from the Kwäday Dän Ts'ìnchi Project**, by Richard J. Hebda, Sheila Greer and Alexander Mackie (Victoria: Royal BC Museum, 2011). This source has plenty of photos and a detailed summary of the discovery and research into Kwäday Dän Ts'ìnchi. Available online only, at https://issuu.com/royalbcmuseum/docs/kdt_highlights.

**Discovering the Inca Ice Maiden**, by Johan Reinhard (Washington, D.C.: National Geographic Society, 1998). An account of the 1995 discovery of three Inca children in Peru, told by one of the men who found them.

# Timeline

| *YBP | Detail | Date |
|---:|---|:---:|
| 2 700 000 | Oldest known ice in Antarctica | 2 700 000 BCE |
| 200 000 | Emergence of *Homo sapiens* (approx.) | 200 000 BCE |
| 45 000 | Mammoth nicknamed Zhenya dies, maybe killed by humans | 43 000 BCE |
| 42 000 | Baby mammoth Lyuba dies in a mud hole in Siberia | 40 000 BCE |
| 39 000 | Yuka, a young mammoth, dies in northern Russia | 37 000 BCE |
| 25 000 | Glacial maximum; dry land exposed in Beringia | 23 000 BCE |
| 12 460 | A puppy dies near a river in northern Russia | 10 450 BCE |
| 12 000 | Two baby cave lions die in a landslide in Russia | 10 000 BCE |
| 12 000 | The glaciers melt, flooding central Beringia | 10 000 BCE |
| 9400 | Earliest Yukon artifacts recovered from ice patches | 7400 BCE |
| 8000 | Carved antler point made and lost on Yukon ice patch | 6000 BCE |
| 5200 | Approximate time Ötzi lived | 3200 BCE |
| 4300 | Yukon dart shaft found by Don Russell is made | 2300 BCE |
| 4200 | Ancient Britons haul huge stones to build Stonehenge | 2150 BCE |
| 2500 | Scythian culture flourishes; kurgans built | 500 BCE |
| 2400 | First Yukon caribou dung sample | 400 BCE |
| 2049 | Beginning of Roman Empire | 31 BCE |
| 2000 | Early scaring-stick hunting in Norway; continued for centuries | 20 CE |
| 1300 | Yukon moccasin lost | 720 CE |
| 1200 | Volcanic eruption creates White River ash | 820 CE |
| 580 | Beginning of Inca Empire | 1438 CE |
| 520 | The Llullaillaco children die (approx.) | 1500 CE |

*YBP means Years Before Present. This is the system scientists use when they talk about how old an artifact is or how long ago something happened, and that's the way radiocarbon dates are expressed. Dates in human history, though, are usually given as CE (Common Era) or BCE (Before Common Era), which refers to the standard calendar used today in most of the world. So, for example, the Inca Empire was founded in 1438 CE. In 2018, that date is 580 YBP.

# Index